SUMMERS MATTER

SUMMERS MATTER

10 Things Every Parent, Teacher, & Principal
Should Know About June, July, & August

By Matthew Boulay, PhD

"There is no off season."
- Nike

"The mind is like a rubber band. If you let it go unused, it gets hard and cracked, and there's no elasticity anymore."

—2nd Grade Mother

"We see summer learning loss in math and in reading. I know our 4th graders, for instance, were struggling with double-digit subtraction when they got back in September. It was like they hadn't done it before."

—Elementary School Principal

CONTENTS

PREFACE: WE AMERICANS LOVE OUR SUMMERS!

"Summertime is always the best of what might be."

—Charles Bowden, Author and Journalist

"America doesn't have a school problem. It has a summer vacation problem."

—Malcolm Gladwell, Author and Journalist

So who's right–Charles Bowden or Malcom Gladwell? Is summertime the best time of the year or are the summer months a problematic and challenging time for children, families and communities?

All of my experiences–as an elementary school teacher in one of the poorest neighborhoods in New York City, as a researcher and academic, as a program provider and summer learning advocate in Baltimore, and, most importantly, now as a father in Oregon–lead me to believe that BOTH are correct!

Across the nation, summers are at once the most enjoyable and the most difficult time of the year.

It's true: We Americans love our summers–and we should! In the best of circumstances, summer is our chance for rest, relaxation, and free time. It's playing in the park and barbecuing at the lake or beach. It's swimming and watermelon and fireworks on the Fourth of July. It's the carefree days we remember from our youth and it's time we can spend now with good friends in good weather. At its best, summer is a delightful rush of family trips, favorite books, overnight camps, late movies, lazy mornings, and warm afternoons.

At the same time, however, the summer months present a unique set of challenges for parents and educators: How do we keep our children safe and supervised when schools are closed but adults still have to work? How do we preserve the academic gains that children achieved during the school year? And, in this age of too many video games and too much junk food, how do we monitor and limit screen time while keeping our kids physically active and eating healthy?

Parents and teachers across the country have wrestled with these questions for decades. The good news is that researchers have quietly amassed a mountain of evidence documenting why summers matter and what we can do as parents and educators to help our children during the months when schools are closed. In short, we now know beyond a shadow of a doubt that what our children do during their summers has a long-term and significant impact on their academic achievement and life chances.

As a sociologist, I know that research evidence matters – but as a parent, I want information to be presented in a simple and straightforward way without confusing academic jargon.

My goal in writing this book has been to act as a kind of translator. In other words, I have taken the most compelling findings from research and translated them into practical guidance for parents, teachers, and principals. It is my hope that this information will not only empower readers to help their own children but spur all of us to think more broadly about the ways in which children experience summer in communities across our entire nation. Ultimately, the challenge of providing summer learning opportunities for ALL children, particularly our most vulnerable, is one that must be taken up by a broad coalition of citizens, educators, child advocates, business leaders, and elected officials.

As a starting point, I hope you find this book both easy-to-read and useful. The sections at the end of the book, "Your FREE Guide to the Twelve Weeks of Summer" and "My Summer Matters! The 20-2-1 Summer Challenge," are designed to be fun and easy tools for you and your family to use throughout the summer.

Finally-and most importantly-I hope that you and the children you know and love have a healthy, smart, and ridiculously wonderful summer!

(1)

Summers Matter
(Much More Than You Think)

WHAT'S THE BIGGEST SLIDE IN AMERICA?

Are you a thrill seeker? One of those people who dreams of going over Niagara Falls in a barrel or parachuting out of an airplane at thirty thousand feet?

If so, you'll love Verruckt. Seventeen stories high, it's steeper than a ski slope and faster than a cheetah. Just 15 minutes from downtown Kansas City, it's the world's tallest waterslide.

But it's not the biggest slide in America.

The biggest slide in America is what social scientists call "the summer slide." Also called "summer setback" or "summer learning loss", this slide is not a joyride. In fact, educational research suggests that summer learning loss is one of the most significant causes of underachievement in America.

SLL = UNDERACHIEVEMENT In

There are 50 million public school students in our country. Each summer, the average American child loses between 1 and 3 MONTHS of learning in reading and math. What does that mean? Here's one way to think about it: If a child gains 9 months of learning during the school year but then loses 3 months of learning during the summer, it's as if the school year is just 6 months long.

The precise amount of summer learning loss varies by child. Children in the younger grades tend to experience much greater loss than children in the older grades, and children living in poverty tend to lose more than their affluent classmates.

To understand summer learning loss, consider this example of a child who takes a test on her first day of first grade. She scores 100 points, which is exactly where her teacher and principal expect her to be as a first grader in September:

September (start of 1st grade): 100 points = ON GRADE LEVEL

Nine months later, she takes another test on the last day of first grade. She's worked hard and it shows: she scores 200 points! Her teacher and parents are thrilled because she gained 100 points during first grade:

June (end of 1st grade): 200 points = GREAT PROGRESS

But then what happens? Well, imagine she is tested three months later on the first day of second grade. On this test, she only scores 170 points:

September (start of 2nd grade): 170 points = DOWN FROM 200

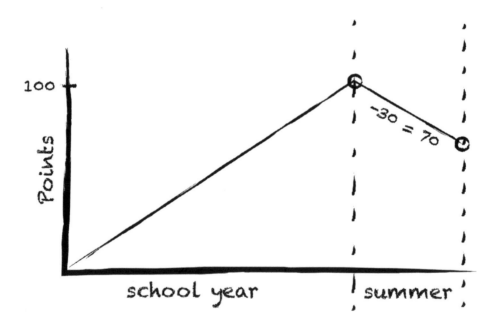

In other words, she dropped 30 points over the summer. It's like she went from an "A" in June to a "C" in September.

	Gains/Losses	Subtotal
First grade	= +100 points	100 points
Summer	= –30 points	70 points

That's summer learning loss. She actually scored lower at the end of the summer than she did just a few months earlier.

Now let's consider a different scenario: Instead of a summer in which she loses 30 points (down to 70 from 100), imagine she gains 30 points. Rather than starting 2nd grade at 70 points, she starts 2nd grade at 130 points!

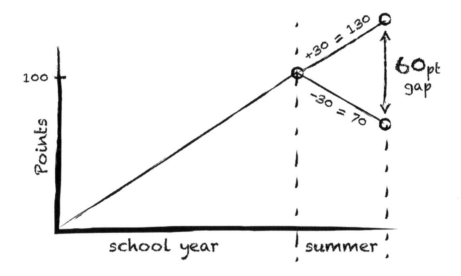

That's quite a difference–and remember, her learning during the school year did not change. The difference between starting second grade at 70 points versus starting at 130 points can be attributed to the learning gains or learning losses that occurred during the summer months when school was closed.

CUMULATIVE MEANS SUMMER AFTER SUMMER AFTER SUMMER AFTER...

For many children this cycle of school year gains followed by summer losses repeats itself year after year.

	Gains/Losses	Subtotal
First grade	= +100 points	
Summer	= −30 points	70 points
Second grade	= +100 points	170 points
Summer	= −30 points	140 points
Third grade	= +100 points	240 points
Summer	= −30 points	210 points

The line looks like this:

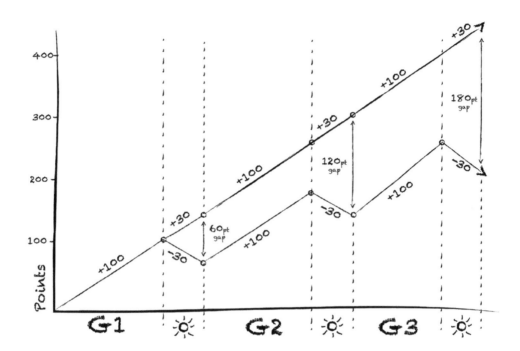

OUR AMAZING BRAINS

The world-renowned physicist Michio Kaku describes the complexity of our brains in beautiful, almost poetic terms:

> *"The human brain has 100 billion neurons, each neuron connected to 10 thousand other neurons. Sitting on your shoulders is the most complicated object in the known universe."*

Consider this: The Library of Congress holds 19 million volumes, totaling more than 10 terabytes of data (that's a million million bytes of data). The human brain's memory capacity is larger than that!

Scientists estimate that a single brain cell can hold 5 times as much information as The Encyclopedia Brittanica!

The brain's capacity to learn is astonishing. Just think of an infant's amazing ability to recognize faces, read expressions, comprehend words and eventually learn to speak, not to mention roll over, crawl and walk. And that's all within just the first year of life.

Of course, with the capacity to learn comes the capacity to forget.

Researchers-and common sense-tells us that we're most likely to forget the skills and content that are the newest and least practiced. This means that children in elementary schools are the most vulnerable to learning loss.

If summer learning matters, then summer learning in the early grades REALLY matters.

"The early period of schooling sets the stage for virtually everything that follows: Achievement patterns and work habits are established, reputations are formed, a paper trail is put in place that will follow children for the rest of their schooling, and children's ideas about self and school begin to crystallize."

—Sociologists Karl Alexander and Doris Entwisle

HOW TO THINK ABOUT LEARNING

LIKE A SOCIOLOGIST

Summer learning loss is a sneaky little devil that does a great job hiding from us.

Most students are tested once a year per state and school district requirements. In other words, school year learning is not separated from summer learning–all 12 months of learning (and forgetting) are jumbled together.

Here's a question that sociologists ask themselves:

If schools are set up to foster learning, what happens to learning when schools are closed?

Researchers have not only asked this question but they've answered it: for most students learning during the summer slows down, slips backwards, or just falls right off the cliff.

THERE'S SCHOOLING, AND THEN THERE'S LEARNING

I like schools and I admire the millions of teachers and principals who commit themselves to our children's learning. In fact, my students used to tease me because I even liked the school food (some of it).

But let's be clear: schooling is not the same thing as learning. Schooling happens from Monday through Friday six hours a day, 180 days a year. By contrast, learning can happen all the time and in many settings. Out-of-school learning experiences can be extraordinarily positive and stimulating. In other words, summers can be a time for children to learn in new and wonderful ways.

This type of learning happens in all kinds of places, such as museums, libraries, parks, and, of course, in homes. Summer can be a time for students to build robots, keep journals, perform plays, create art, listen to stories, explore nature, and ask questions.

Parents can do many things to support learning in their own homes, such as practicing math while cooking together or acting out stories that children have read (the "Guide" and "Challenge" at the end of this book provide many more tips and suggestions). In addition, there may be places in your community with free or low-cost opportunities and resources that help children have fun, be safe, and learn new things during the summer.

Across the nation, public libraries and parks typically offer summer activities, as do organizations such as the YMCA and Boys and Girls Clubs of America.

Here are a few more ideas:

- If you go to baseball games, ask your child to count the innings, the number of foul balls, or strikes;
- When you are preparing dinner, have your child read the ingredients and directions out loud to you;
- If you go on a walk, ask your child about what they see, hear, smell, and experience; and
- Practice language skills by taking turns talking at dinner;

Summer learning isn't about just adding more things to your already full to-do list! And it's important to point out that parents alone are not responsible for changing the way that children experience summer. Many big and small changes in our country need to happen to make it easier to provide safe and healthy learning environments throughout your communities and throughout the year.

In short, parents can't control what children are taught in school, but we can have a large impact on the content of learning opportunities in the summers. Given the degree to which the curriculum of public schools has narrowed due to focus on testing, this attitude is important–we can think of summers as a time to customize our children's education. Summers are a particularly good opportunity to take into account our children's interests and likes–building activities around what our children enjoy or want to explore is essential to creating positive summer learning experiences.

John Lennon once said, "There are no problems. Only solutions." Our job–and the purpose of this book–is to show how we can transform the problem of summer learning loss into the joy and opportunity of summer learning.

LET'S END THIS CHAPTER WITH
AN IMPORTANT DISCLAIMER

Now that I've introduced the notion of summer learning loss and provided some of the research evidence suggesting that summers really do matter, I want to pause for a moment to clarify what I mean by summer learning.

I know from experiences that when I talking about "summer learning" many people hear "summer school." Those two words–"summer" and "school"–are not popular when uttered together. They invoke images of unhappy students being forced to endure boring classes in hot classrooms with unloving teachers and no joy. For most people, the idea of summer learning conjures unpleasant words like "punitive," "remedial," and "mandatory."

So, let's pause for these disclaimers:

1. When I say "summer learning" I do not mean "summer school;"
2. I am NOT the Grinch who stole summer vacation; and
3. I think summers are the BEST time to engage children and nurture creativity. Summers are the time when learning is free from the demands of testing and textbooks; in other words, summers are the ideal time for children to learn and explore new interests in wonderful ways that are so fun they seem to have nothing to do with learning or schooling.

> *"Summer afternoon—summer afternoon; to me those have always been the two most beautiful words in the English language."*
>
> **—Henry James**

CHAPTER 1 POP-QUIZ

1. **On average, how much learning does the average American child lose every summer?**
2. **Summer learning is the same as summer school. (Circle: True or False)**
3. **Summer learning should be _____. (Fill in the blank)**

②

The Art of
Off-Season Training:
Advice From The Pros

Imagine your favorite team. They've had a good season but now it's over. After their last game you are in the locker room listening to the coach say something like this:

"I'm proud of you – every single one of you. I asked you for 100 percent, and you gave me a 110 percent! You've played hard every minute of every game. Now our season is over and I want all of you to kick back and do nothing for the off-season. Don't work out. Don't train. Don't study the playbook. Take it easy. Eat donuts, drink sugary drinks, play video games and take a long break. We'll have plenty of time next season to get our bodies back into shape. Any questions? Ok, then, 'til we see each other next season. And remember, do nothing. ABSOLUTELY NOTHING!"

I don't think so.

Coaches don't tell their players to quit training during the off-season. They tell them to KEEP TRAINING. Every sport has an off-season and every ambitious athlete, coach and personal fitness trainer knows that the off-season presents a special opportunity to develop strength, skills, and stamina. Basketball coach and author Tony Alfonso put it this way: "The great players show how much they want to play during the offseason–when it's hot, when it's tough, and when no one is watching."

Here are some other nuggets of wisdom about training in the off-season:

"Don't take the off-season lightly, because you have the chance to come back stronger, faster, more explosive and better than you have ever been."

—Conor Doherty, Personal Trainer

"You could argue that off-season training is the most important phase of any sport-specific conditioning plan. Not only will it help the athlete to recover physically and psychologically, it can be used to address some of the physical imbalances that are inherent with playing competitive sport."

—SportsFitnessAdvisor.com

"The game of soccer is incredibly demanding. You must be able to sprint, explode to the ball and change direction – and maintain these skills for a long duration. So, to improve your game on the pitch, you must develop your overall athleticism, including strength, speed, power and endurance. And the best time to do this is during the off-season."

Stack Magazine

THE OFF-SEASON IS AN OPPORTUNITY TO GET AHEAD

Yael Averbuch is a professional soccer player with FC Kansas City and has played on the United States women's national soccer team since 2013. Yael might not be a household name (yet!) but she's a brilliant soccer player as well as one of the hardest working and most disciplined athletes I've ever seen. As a college player, she set the record for the number of consecutive games started: 105! Take a look at her photo and you'll see what I mean.

With an inch of snow on the ground, and more falling, Yael is practicing dribbling–one of the most fundamental skills in the game of soccer.

In addition to her full-time career as a professional athlete, Yael is a prolific writer and advocate for children's health. Her blog is full of smart tips and she recently published an op-ed in the New York Times called, "The Art of Off-Season Training." Take a look at how she thinks about training in the off-season:

"Much of the preparation for the season takes place in the long offseason."

"My main goals this off-season are to improve my strength and speed and to reach a new level of fitness."

"For those of us who truly embrace the off-season, it can be one of the most meaningful parts of our playing career–a time like no other to take personal responsibility for improvement and to savor the joy of just playing."

"For those of us who aspire to be the best we can be, there is technically never an off-season. For me at least, the downtime between seasons is part of a continuous cycle of improvement.

"I think of the off-season as a blank canvas. I can recreate myself as a player, fine-tune areas of my game, sharpen my strengths and attack my weaknesses head-on. It is when I improve most, by taking my development back to the basics, far from the spotlight of games or organized team training sessions."

Yael is serious about the offseason but she's clearly not alone. Other elite athletes like tennis great Serena Williams and basketball star LeBron James approach the off-season with the same serious attitude:

Serena maintains a strict diet, runs hills and plays tennis three to four hours a day during the off-season.

LeBron lifts weights, runs, and plays basketball during the off-season even after winning back-to-back championships.

Athletes like Yael, Serena and LeBron know that winning during the regular season depends on how they train during the off-season. They set goals for themselves and develop a training plan to meet those goals.

Of course, it's certainly true that all of us need time for rest and relaxation. Children, in particular, need a break from the demands of formal schooling. No child, however, should take a break from learning. Our brains are like the muscles of those elite athletes: when properly exercised, they grow strong; when ignored, they shrink and become weak.

In other words, it's use it or lose it.

"By the time I sat down to write "Family Pictures," I hadn't written anything in almost two years and writing, I have discovered, is a muscle: if it isn't exercised, it will atrophy."

—Bestselling author Jane Green (her books have sold millions of copies and been translated into more than 25 languages)

USE THE OFF-SEASON TO TRAIN DIFFERENTLY

While it's true that athletes train hard in the offseason it's also true that their off-season training programs are different from what their workouts during the regular season. In the same way, our goals and plans for summer learning can be different than what happens during the school year. For example, subjects like art and science that are difficult to fit in during the school year can be great activities during the summer months.

Remember, you don't have to teach your child trigonometry or a new language during the summer. The goal is simply keep your child's mind engaged. For some children, summer can be a time for catching up and reinforcing skills that may not have been mastered in the previous year, but summer learning should be balanced with activities that your child really loves and wants to do.

SPECIAL SNEAK PREVIEW: The last section of this book is the 20-2-1 Summer Challenge. Jump ahead if you want to start setting goals and making a plan for your summer learning.

(3)

Summer Learning is NOT Summer School

SUMMER LEARNING

MATTERS, NOW WHAT?"

Nearly every family in America confronts the age-old question of what to do for the summer. As the mother of a second grader recently told me, "I want my daughter to have a good summer but what does that mean, and how can I help her?" Here's the simple, most important answer: summer learning should be fun learning.

THE "OTHER" GOLDEN RULE: WHEN IT COMES TO SUMMER LEARNING, DON'T BE EVIL!

Fifteen years ago, I was teaching fourth grade in an elementary school in New York City. As I was telling the class that I would be absent the next day because I needed to attend a conference on summer learning, one of my students, a quiet little girl in the front row, shook her head in a sad and disapproving way. When I asked her what was wrong, she said, "Mr. Boulay, summer school? That's evil."

"The best way to make children good is to make them happy."

—Oscar Wilde, author and poet

BUST THAT MYTH!

The National Summer Learning Association, the non-profit organization I started in 1992, gives an award each year called the Excellence in Summer Learning Award. Sarah Pitcock, the CEO of NSLA, described these by saying that they, "Bust the myth that summer learning is boring or punitive by offering some of the most engaging, individualized and hands-on learning opportunities available to young people today."

Our challenge is to keep our child's brain awake and humming all summer long. There are a thousand ways to do this, and many free resources to help you. Summer learning can be grouped into three broad categories: enrollment-based programs such as camps, drop-in programs like the public library, and at-home learning that can take place anytime and anywhere.

❏ Enrollment-Based Programs
"Summer learning programs have the potential to help children and youth improve academic and other outcomes...

Students need to attend regularly, and programming needs to be high-quality and aligned with student needs. Research indicates that several factors may be related to improved program effectiveness, including provision of individualized instruction, parental involvement, and small class sizes."

—**"Making Summer Count"**
published by The RAND Corporation, 2011

❏ Drop-In Programs

"I received the fundamentals of my education in school, but that was not enough. My real education, the superstructure, the details, the true architecture, I got out of the public library. For an impoverished child whose family could not afford to buy books, the library was the open door to wonder and achievement, and I can never be sufficiently grateful that I had the wit to charge through that door and make the most of it."

—Isaac Asimov, Scientist and Author

❏ At-Home Learning

"Children learn from anything and everything they see. They learn wherever they are, not just in special learning places."

—John Holt, Former Schoolteacher & Author "How Children Learn" and "How Children Fail"

SUMMER IS A GOOD TIME
TO FAIL, REALLY!

Unfortunately, the word failure has become synonymous with under-performance or the absence of learning. However, a friend who teaches middle school science likes to tell her students that it is not only okay to fail, it's necessary to fail! The scientific process relies on hypothesis testing, experimentation, and the search for empirical evidence–all of which consider "failure" to be an important part of the learning process.

Jules Verne, the author of "Twenty Thousand Leagues Under the Sea" and "Around the World in Eighty Days," said, "Science is made up of mistakes, but they are mistakes which it is useful to make, because they lead little by little to the truth." And Bram Stoker, the author of "Dracula," said it this way:

"We learn from failure, not from success."

Away from grades and tests and the other pressures of the school year, summer can be a safe place for children to "fail." As long as parents and caring adults are around to support them, it's great to encourage your children to experiment by exploring new subjects and areas of interest.

MANAGING SCREEN TIME

Depending on the age and interests of your child, there is much that children can learn through a screen. For instance, the non-profit Khan Academy offers a free online program that introduces children to the fundamentals of coding. It's self-paced and quite amazing. For older youth, the New York Times posts short videos on subjects that range from science to art and literature to current affairs.

> *"Content matters. The quality of content is more important than the platform or time spent with media. Prioritize how your child spends his time rather than just setting a timer."*
> **—The American Academy of Pediatrics**

Thousands of websites and television shows nurture children's creativity and stimulate their thinking. They key is to use screens in conjunction with reading, not as a substitute for it. In other words, don't use media as a cheap and convenient "electronic babysitter." It's always important to talk with your child about what they are watching in order to help them make sense of the content and to answer their questions. And, of course, monitor what they watch-a lot of online content is violent, unsavory and not healthy or safe for children.

In short, experts generally say that it's ok for children to use screens in a <u>limited</u> way as long as they are <u>supervised</u>. A little bit of "down time" or "taking a break" is fine but playing video games or watching television for hours is a "brain drain."

FOR MORE TIPS AND GUIDANCE:

The University of Michigan Health System maintains a website that offers terrific guidance for parents trying to manage TV:

http://www.med.umich.edu/yourchild/topics/managetv.htm

4

A Bedtime Story?
YES!

A Bedtime Math Problem?
ARE YOU NUTS?

What does bedtime look like in your home during the school year? Probably something like this: brush teeth, put on pajamas, read a story, then give a goodnight kiss and lights out.

And what does bedtime look like in the summer months? Does your child protest, "But it's still light out! I'm not tired! I don't want to go to bed yet!"

KEEP YOUR GOOD HABITS

Children and families develop many good habits during the school year that are important to maintain during the summer months. For example, from September to May children are used to doing homework on a nightly or weekly basis. While homework isn't assigned during the summer months, the habit of setting aside time for learning is a very good one. Here are three quick tips:

❑ If you read to your child at bedtime during the school year, read to him or her during the summer.

❑ If you limit and monitor screen time during the school year, limit and monitor screen time during the summer.

❑ If you keep a regular bedtime schedule during the school year, do the same during the summer.

ROUTINE, ROUTINE, ROUTINE,

I know that as parents we can sometimes feel overwhelmed. For example, when asked about the summer, one frustrated parent said, "My kids go to bed anytime...nothing's ever at the same time every day."

It's true that children tend to stay up later during the summer months. For example, I live in Salem, Oregon, where it can stay light outside until nearly 10 pm. While it's fine to gently relax the rules a bit during the summer months, it's helpful to maintain a routine. And, of course, it's important that children still get between 8 and 10 hours of sleep each night.

LET YOUR CHILD READ WHATEVER
WHEREVER WHENEVER!

"There is no such thing as a child who hates to read; there are only children who have not found the right book."

—Frank Serafini
Children's Author & Professor of Education Literacy

When I was in 4th grade, my teacher assigned Mark Twain's classic, "The Adventures of Huckleberry Finn." Ernest Hemingway hailed it as a the "one book" from which "all modern American literature" came, and critics still consider it to be one of the most important books written by an American. It's a delightful story that can be read on many levels – as an entertaining series of youthful adventures and mishaps, and as a devastatingly clever critique of racism. As a 4th grader, however, it was too difficult for me. I struggled with the vocabulary and Twain's vernacular style. In fact, I struggled so much that I became frustrated-sadly, I used to tell people that I hated Twain's famous book.

My story highlights the difference between school year reading and summer reading. Whereas we expect teachers to introduce students to different authors and genres, summer reading is WIDE OPEN. As long as children are reading at least 20 minutes a day, five days a week (or more!) let them read anything they want (of course, it should be age appropriate).

My nine-year old daughter has a few favorites that she reads again and again. During the school year, her teacher encourages her to branch out and try some new things. But over the summer, we let her read anything she wants, even if it's the same book over and over. In fact, some experts suggest that reading the same book again and again is important because it allows children to deepen their experience by reading it repeatedly.

MAKE FRIENDS WITH NUMBERS

While many families know that it's important to read during the summer months, it's easy to think that math is a "school thing" which doesn't need to be practiced during the summer. When asked about learning over the summer, one parent told me, "The only thing that drops off is we don't do as much math." A recent edition of the magazine Science published a study on the benefits of practicing math at home:

> *"Most parents understand that to help their children develop academically they should read to them," says Sian Beilock, a cognitive psychologist at the University of Chicago in Illinois and an author of the new study [on Bedtime Math]. But parents often assume that the school will take care of math instruction, she notes. "Our hope is that this study helps change the notion that math is the purview of the school and shows that talking about math at home is helpful," Beilock says.*

Just as it is important to continue to read during the summer, it's important for your child to keep his or her math skills sharp. To help you get started, Bedtimemath.org is a terrific website run by a nonprofit organization started by Laura Overdeck, an astrophysicist trained at Princeton. Parents love the site. There are already over 200,000 users from all 50 states! Here's how one parent described getting started:

> *"My daughter was annoyed the first night I introduced this to her bedtime routine, accepting the second night, and by the third night*

she wanted math before her story. It has completely transformed my daughter's attitude towards math."

Laura told me the story of one mother whose children grew to love Bedtime Math so much that she used it as a threat to get them moving at bedtime.

"If you don't get your teeth brushed in the next three minutes, no math tonight!"

—Elisa K.

A team of researchers studied the benefits of practicing daily math at home during the school year and found that "over the course of one 9-month school year, students who do bedtime math gain on average the equivalent of a 3-month advantage over their peers."

Finally, it's important to acknowledge that a lot of us feel some anxiety about math. One mother recently told me, "I'm terrible at math. I don't wanna teach it wrong." If you feel this kind math anxiety, talk with your child's teacher. He or she can provide some guidance that is appropriate for your child's age and ability level, and many schools have subscriptions to online math programs that can be used during the summer months.

In addition to BedtimeMath.org, there are many free websites where children of every age and ability level can find practice problems and instructional videos. Two of the most popular are KhanAcademy.org and PatrickJMT.com.

AND WRITE!

I recently met a young mother who dropped out of high school. Full of regrets for not going further with her own education, she and her husband are now determined that their children succeed in school. When I asked how she supported them during the summer months, she said that she required them to do chores every day and to write in a journal every day. Her secret, she says, it to give her children the flexibility to write as much or as little as they'd like, and to write on whatever topic interest them – but to insist that they write every day:

> *"Sometimes it would be just a few sentences with a picture. Other times, it would be a whole page of sentences and a picture on the next one. It depended on what we did that day, what they felt like they wanted to write down. It could range anywhere between 10 minutes to a good half-hour to 45 minutes if they were really into it."*

A FEW TIPS FOR FUN SUMMER WRITING

Many parents encourage their children to write letters over the summer to their favorite authors, athletes, actors, and singers. You can also write to the President of the United States of America, and to governors, senators and representatives. In almost all cases, these entertainers and elected officials will write back, which can be great fun for your children.

Writing so-called "fan fiction" can also be a blast. Take a character from a favorite book or movie and extend the story. Depending on your children's ages and interests, challenge them to create a new adventure for Dora the Explorer or for Superman, or to make up their own funny story about Greg from "Diary of a Wimpy Kid."

(5)

Food Also Matters.
And Exercise!
And Sleep!!

"Take care of your body. It's the only place you have to live."

—Jim Rohn, Author and Entrepreneur

We've talked about how summer learning is NOT summer school. Let's take it a step further. Summer learning is also not exclusively about your child's mind. Today more than ever we understand that body and mind are linked – healthy habits are absolutely crucial to preventing summer learning loss.

SUMMERTIME WEIGHT GAIN

This might surprise you, but researchers have recently discovered that the summer months can be a particularly unhealthy time of year for many children:

"Children gain weight two or three times faster during summer vacation than during the school year."

**—Paul von Hippel, PhD,
Researcher, Ohio State University**

Findings such as this are particularly troubling because rates of childhood obesity have tripled over the past 40 years. Poor nutrition and physical inactivity during the summers can lead to the type of weight gain that puts children and youth at risk for high cholesterol, high blood pressure, type 2 diabetes, joint problems, and social and psychological problems including stigmatization, bullying and poor self-esteem. It's a problem that can have major implications for learning:

"Childhood obesity may be associated with compromised academic performance and cognitive functioning, such as impaired planning, inhibition, and problem solving skills."

**—Researchers Amy Bohnert,
Nicole Zarrett, and Amy Mahoney**

While all of us would like to believe that summers are a time in which the warm weather and long days allow children to increase their physical activity, the reality is that for many children summers are time without a daily schedule or structure. In turn, that means that children eat more junk food, play more video games, and exercise less than during the school year. Indeed, one parent recently told me, "When you're talking about summer health and nutrition, parents seem to agree that diet and daily routines change in the summer, often for the worse. Ice cream every night, a lot of unstructured time that often turns into screen time. While downtime can be great in moderation, it's not a good thing in excess."

AND SUMMERTIME HUNGER

And here's another surprise: while some kids gain too much weight during the summers, others don't have enough to eat and experience summertime hunger. Indeed, six out of seven children who qualify for federally funded meals when school is in session don't have access to those meals during the summer. Put differently, only one in seven of the low-income children who rely on school lunch during the school year participated in the summer meals program. As advocates for these children say, "Hunger doesn't take a summer vacation."

The good news is that the federal summer meals program is available to schools, programs and communities across the country. The U.S. Department of Agriculture administers summer meals and you can get more information from your state department of education, member of Congress, or the Department of Agriculture's website.

EAT HEALTHY

"Over the course of a year, children ages 2–7 see an average of 4,427 food ads."

—The Kaiser Family Foundation

We all know that eating healthy is important, but it's not always easy. As the quote above makes clear, all of us–including our children-are constantly bombarded with advertisements for sugary drinks, fast food and junk food. And, of course, the junk food industry receives millions of dollars in federal grants and subsidies–in fact, subsidies for the junk food industry have gone up while funding for summer learning programs has gone down!

What can you do in your own home during the summer? As a starting point, eat meals WITH your child as often as you can–but WITHOUT the TV. That way, instead of getting bombarded with all those ads, you'll have a chance to talk as a family.

And while we've heard it all before, the experts' guidelines are worth repeating: Eat fruits and vegetables, drink water and beverages without added sugars, and eat minimally processed foods made with whole grains and, heart-healthy oils/fats, and without added sugar or trans-fats.

HEALTHY BODY, HEALTHY MIND

President Kennedy said, "Physical fitness is not only one of the most important keys to a healthy body, it is the basis of dynamic and creative intellectual activity."

The summer months are the perfect time for outdoor play and physical activity. As adults, we cherish summertime memories–for me and my siblings, it was endless hours of tag, climbing trees, swimming, and staying up late to catch fireflies. Unfortunately, things are different for many children today. A number of factors conspire to keep kids indoors, including parental concerns about safety, the popularity of video games, and, in general, too few community resources. Many parents tell me, for example, that they would love for their children's school–particularly the school library and gym-to be open during the summer months. It's in the neighborhood, it's safe, and all of the books and basketball hoops are already there and paid for!

INACTIVITY, BOREDOM AND

LOW SELF-ESTEEM

For some children, the summer months are a time when they watch more television, spend less time conversing with adults, and experience less parental involvement in their day-to-day-lives.

Social scientists suggest that boredom and alienation characterize the summertime experience for many youth, particularly those who are not in structured programs.

"Watching television and other unstructured, passive activities are associated with higher levels of alienation and lower levels of challenge, positive affect, and attention/concentration.

—Researcher Amy Bohnert

EXERCISE!

Most experts recommend that children exercise at least sixty minutes a day!

Make it fun. As an adult, if you've ever tried to incorporate exercise into your routine, you know that it won't last long if it's not fun. The same is true for kids. So mix it up. Change the setting. Think about "alternative" ways to exercise such as swimming or romping around a pool. For younger kids, play tag; for older kids, hike.

SLEEP!

"Sleep helps your brain work properly."
                    —**The National Institutes of Health**

With more hours of daylight in the summer months, children tend to go to bed later and sleep less. Unhealthy levels of weight gain are associated with sleep deficiencies–in other words, as children sleep less, they tend to experience unhealthy levels of weight gain. There are also other significant effects of not getting enough sleep:

> *"Children and teens who are sleep deficient may have problems getting along with others. They may feel angry and impulsive, have mood swings, feel sad or depressed, or lack motivation. They also may have problems paying attention, and they may get lower grades & feel stressed."*
>   —**National Institutes of Health**

We also know that physical activity improve the quality of sleep. When kids are sitting on the couch all day, they may not sleep as well–and then the following day they will be too tired to get off the couch; it's a vicious cycle that adequate exercise can help avoid.

In sum, the studies don't lie: With obesity rates skyrocketing and summer learning loss closely associated with the health of our children, we are seeing the effects of inactive summers all across America. It's useful to remember that all of these pieces are connected: An active body fosters an active mind; Better sleep means a more active body and mind; and Healthy eating habits feeds body and mind as well.

Urge your elected officials to increase the number of programs that are available during the summer and to support local libraries and schools that already offer summer activities.

POP-QUIZ

Directions: Circle the correct answer.

My goals for the summer are:

A. To keep reading
B. To practice math
C. To have fun
D. All of the Above!

⑥

Middle School Students Are _____.
(FiLL IN THE BLANK)

"Nothing could be as hard as middle school."

—Zooey Deschanel, Actress

"I've never run into a person who yearns for their middle school days."

—Jeff Kinney, Author of the "Diary of a Wimpy Kid" series

NO DOUBT ABOUT IT, THE MIDDLE SCHOOL YEARS CAN BE DIFFICULT

Middle school students are too old for elementary school and too young for high school, which leaves them where? No one is quite sure – I guess that's why they invented middle school.

Even pop stars can have a tough time in middle school:

> "A lot of people ask me, 'How did you have the courage to walk up to record labels when you were 12 or 13 and jump right into the music industry?' It's because I knew I could never feel the kind of rejection that I felt in middle school. Because in the music industry, if they're gonna say no to you, at least they're gonna be polite about it."
>
> **—Taylor Swift**

Middle school youth are like elementary children except that they're older, moodier, needier, more mature, less mature, more confident, more self-conscious, and so on.

In other words, middle school students are full of contradictions. They are at once ridiculously rebellious towards us as parents and, simultaneously, deeply in need of our love and approval.

Developmentally, we can think of pre-school children as "home children" and elementary schoolers as "school children," middle schoolers are just becoming children of their communities-but many of the same lessons from their younger years still apply. The good news is that by the time they've reached middle school many children often have the maturity and discipline to pursue an area of interest and explore it in depth. That one reason that many of the best summer programs for middle school students employ inquiry-based and project-based learning.

THEY STILL NEED YOU (EVEN IF IT DOESN'T SEEM LIKE IT)

"There were times when, in middle school and junior high, I didn't have a lot of friends. But my mom was always my friend. Always."

—Taylor Swift

Your middle school child still needs you and your endless font of parental love and support. I know, I know, it's not easy–but it's true. They need you to talk with them and to listen to them. And summer is a great time to do this.

Middle school can also be a fun time. It's a time when kids become aware of the world around them, and a time of many "firsts."

"My first dunk ever was in middle school. We were playing, me and my church friends, and I dunked it, and I swear I could not sleep that night."

—Jeremy Lin, NBA star

As children get older, self-regulation and choice are very important – and should play a role is designing their summer experiences. In other words, by middle school, parents should be listening carefully to their child and working together to build a plan for the summer.

SUPERVISION STILL MATTERS - BUT IT'S TRICKY

As children get older it is, of course, true that dangers lurk. They may start to smoke, or experiment with drugs and alcohol. The summer months can be a more dangerous time because middle and high school youth tend to have more free time and less adult supervision. Researchers have found that middle school and high school youth who are involved in summer programs tend to get into less trouble than their classmates who have nothing to do all summer.

Monitor and limit texting, video games, and screens. Your middle schooler won't thank you for it, but it's important to continue to monitor screen time. Some is okay, too much is too much. It's good to have some time in which no screens are allowed–that's tough for many adults AND kids but great for family time.

KEEP READING. KEEP READING.

KEEP READING.

Bestselling author James Patterson has written 147 novels that have been translated into dozens of languages and sold more than 300 million copies worldwide. Yes, that's 300 million!

Patterson's passion is middle school reading. One of his most recent books is titled, "Middle School: The Worst Years of My life." It's a funny book, geared towards middle schoolers. He puts it like this:

> *"What I'm really addicted to is getting people to understand that if their kids aren't competent readers coming out of middle school, it's really going to be hard for them in high school."*

The good news is that there is a ton of new literature geared towards middle school students and young adults. Some of it is very popular, like "The Giver" and "The Hunger Game" series. These books treat young adult readers as if they are adults–the characters are well developed, the plots are complex, and the themes are sophisticated and interesting.

LOOKING AHEAD...WHAT ABOUT THE HIGH SCHOOL YEARS?

At some point in the near future, your little ones will grow up and become big ones. What to do with them in high school? In general, the same principles apply: be there to talk with them, especially during the summer and, if nothing else, keep them reading.

It's really important, especially as kids get older, to take into account their interests and likes and dislikes. Paying attention to your child and what he or she wants to get better at or to explore is essential to creating a positive summer.

I remember only too well, signing up my daughter for a soccer program without asking her about it first. She hated it and, ultimately, my wife and I agreed that she didn't have to go. She was unhappy and it was clearly a bad match.

And, for many high school students, working a summer job will be a priority. That's a good thing, just be sure that their work schedule doesn't interfere too much with their sleep, schoolwork, athletics, or other activities.

SOME GUIDING PRINCIPLES

Researchers at the National Summer Learning Association (NSLA) recently interviewed award-winning summer programs for middle and high school youth and found some common characteristics. These tips can be helpful when you are looking for programs and for ways to connect with your middle school student during the summer months. The most successful programs are:

1. Intellectually Challenging
2. Relevant
   a. Relate to youths' lives and interests
   b. Talk about technology, careers, college
3. Respectful, Fun and Enthusiastic
   a. Fun and supportive
   b. Promoting a sense of success, accomplishment and confidence

Obviously, summer often needs to be the time for catching up and reinforcing skills that may not have been mastered in the previous year, but it should be balanced with activities that the child really loves–this is true for younger children as well as older ones. As I said before, allowing kids to have a say–which should increase as they get older–helps them understand that they are in charge of their own learning.

⑦

If You're a Teacher, Principal or Superintendent, Summer is Gonna Get You Fired!

"We have amazing teachers... and it's extremely disappointing when we just pour everything, our heart and soul, everything, all of us, the whole school, into getting the students to a certain point at the end of the year-and then they come back in the fall and we assess them and they've lost ground."

—Elementary School Principal

TEACHERS ALREADY KNOW ABOUT

SUMMER LEARNING LOSS

Summer learning loss is not news to teachers. In a 2013 survey of 500 teachers by the National Summer Learning Association,

❏ Nearly 66 percent reported needing to devote 3–4 weeks to reviewing or re-teaching the same material at the beginning of the school year that their students had learned the previous spring.

❏ Another 24 percent reported spending five weeks or more backtracking before deciding it was safe to proceed to new terrain.

This means that during a 40-week academic calendar, teachers have to spend more than 10 percent of it pulling their students back up to where they had been before summer slide.

TEACHERS WHO LOOP ARE MOST FAMILIAR WITH SLL

Sometimes called "multi-year grouping", looping is the practice of having a teacher advance to the next grade along with his or her students. For example, Mrs. Jones is a first grade teacher with a classroom of 25 students. In the following school year she would teach second grade to the same group of 25 students.

A teacher in Baltimore once told me that "teachers who loop understand summer learning loss better than anyone because they know exactly what their students learned the previous school year and exactly where each student performed at the end of the previous school year. When the kids come back in September, looping teachers know exactly how much their students lost over the summer." Equally important, looping teachers can "keep the ball rolling" during summer break, using summer reading lists, mini-projects, and field trips.

SLL UNDERCUTS THE WAY
WE LOOK AT SCHOOLS

To put it bluntly, who gets blamed for summer learning loss?

In most states and districts, schools have been judged on test scores under the requirements of No Child Left Behind. Because these tests are administered once a year, school year gains are mixed in with summer losses. Remember the example in Chapter One of the student who gained 100 points during the school year but then lost 30 points during the summer? If the accountability system requires the student to gain 80 points but the net result after summer learning loss is only 70 points, then the student is categorized as underperforming. If there are too many students in this situation, the school is put on a watch list.

In other words, achievement gains made during the school year are undercut by losses that occur during the summer. It's unfair, but politicians and the media often blame schools and teachers for the learning loss that occurs when schools are closed for summer.

Here's what makes it even sadder: Americans seem to be losing confidence in our system of public schools:

"Historical results from Gallup polls show that the percentage of Americans expressing a 'great deal' of confidence in public schools has

declined from 30% in 1973 to only 12% in 2014. Similarly, the percentage of those indicating 'very little' confidence has tied the all-time high of 28% (this figure was reported in both 2012 and 2014 Gallup results)."

Dissatisfaction comes from many areas, but one very important factor is the misunderstanding that occurs when summer learning loss is confounded with school year gains.

OUR MOST VULNERABLE STUDENTS

Three groups of students – those who receive special education services, those living in poverty, and those who are English Language Learners– are particularly vulnerable to summer learning loss. Schools and districts typically devote extra resources these students but summer learning loss undercuts those efforts.

Students with Disabilities

While evidence suggests that children with intellectual, developmental and behavioral disabilities may learn at different rates and in different ways than their classmates without disabilities, little is known about how they and their parents navigate the months away from schooling. Nor, for that matter, do we know whether children with disabilities experience summer learning loss at rates greater than their classmates without disabilities. Further, while extended school year services can be provided during the summer as part of a child's individualized education program (IEP), to my knowledge summer learning research has not focused on these services and their potential impact on children's summer learning outcomes.

Students Living in Poverty

For schools that serve large numbers of children living in poverty, the downward pull of summer learning loss is most extreme. In fact, sociologists have described summer as the most unequal time in America. While well-off families are able to send their children to camps or take them on family vacations, children living in poverty often have few resources available outside of the regular school year. One team of researchers put it this way:

> "Socioeconomic learning disparities grow faster during the summer than they do during the school year."

ELL Students

Given the possibility that their exposure to written and spoken English is limited when away from school, we might expect that English Language Learners are likely to experience extreme summer slide in verbal skills. There are, however, virtually no seasonal studies that address the question.

HERE'S THE BOTTOM LINE...

Most districts operate on the traditional 9-month, 180-day school calendar. As a result, most educators don't think of themselves as "owning" the summer months. The influential school reformer and philosopher John Dewey said in 1916, "If we teach today's students as we taught yesterday's, we rob them of tomorrow."

As a former elementary school teacher myself, I can understand the frustration. Schools are closed for the summer-so it doesn't seem fair to get blamed for summer learning loss.

TEACHER GUIDANCE ABOUT THE SUMMER IS VERY IMPORTANT

"The teachers talked about how if you don't do anything during the summer you will slide back, your skills will need to be re-sharpened in the fall, and you start out behind. So that sunk in for me."
—Mother of a Kindergartener & a 2nd Second Grader

Teachers play a critical–yet often unrecognized–role in shaping parental expectations around summer learning. Some researchers describe teachers as "information brokers" who help parents shape their goals for summer learning and also identify resources in their community that can facilitate summer learning. Here are some tips for teachers:

❏ Help your students' parents think about the resources in their homes and community that might be available during the summer. For example, some schools schedule parent-teacher conversations in May as a way to set goals for summer reading and learning activities.

❏ Make sure that every child has a library card and help parents think about transportation options to and from the local public library.

❏ Try keeping your school's library open during the summer months. Even if it is just for a few hours a day once a week, this allows kids to walk to their neighborhood school to get books on a regular basis.

❏ Many schools subscribe to online learning programs during the school year. Programs like IXL, First in Math, Bedtime Math, RAZ Readers, and many more. These subscriptions are often 12 months long but teachers and parents are frequently unaware that they are available during the summer. Check to see if your online learning program is available during the summer and, if so, make sure your parents know about it.

❏ Give reading lists. Some schools have parents sign "Summer Reading Contracts" to commit to supporting summer reading.

❏ Use data to track your students' summer learning. Talk with your principal to see what data can be easily collected. And help parents track their own children's activities: if they are not enrolled in an organized summer learning program, students or parents may be able to get a summer reading log from their public library to keep track of the time they spend reading during the summer.

❏ Stay in touch with students throughout the summer. Some teachers email their students, some use interactive programs like Google Docs to share stories or poems, some send their students a postcard or two to check in throughout the summer. Just a simple reminder that says, "Hi there, thinking of you. Hope you're reading."

Principals and other school leaders also play an important role. Here are some tips for administrators:

❏ Keep your school library open.

❏ In less affluent areas, keep your cafeteria open. Take advantage of the federal government's summer food program.

❏ If possible, open your gym at least once a week to give children a safe place in the neighborhood to run around and play games.

❏ Explore giving some teachers the opportunity to loop.

❏ Explore ways to track summer learning loss in your school.

❏ Encourage your teachers to talk with parents about summer learning loss and the importance of summer reading.

❏ Partner with local community groups to run summer programs at your school.

❏ Advocate for summer funding. Most state and federal education funding can be used during the summer – an "allowable" use – but it seems the school year always takes priority.

SUPPORT YOUNG PEOPLE'S GROWTH AND DEVELOPMENT THROUGHOUT THE YEAR!

During the school year, we spend nine months nurturing our children's growth and development. As parents and teachers, we dedicate ourselves to helping our children learn and succeed every day they attend school. As a nation, we devote enormous resources to schools because we believe, collectively, that education is the key to opportunity.

Why would we back away from these commitments for three months each year? We should let policy makers know that summer needs to be an integral part of an excellent public education. And meanwhile, there are plenty of things that teachers and school administrators can do to fight summer learning loss. Don't let summer get you fired!

"Teaching is not a lost art, but the regard for it is a lost tradition."

—Jacques Barzun,
Historian & Philosopher of Education

8

If You're Innovative or Creative, Summer is the BEST Time to Innovate and Create

"One of the only ways to get out of a tight box is to invent your way out"
—Jeff Bezos,
Founder and CEO of Amazon.com

"It isn't all over; everything has not been invented; the human adventure is just beginning."

—Gene Roddenberry, Screenwriter,
Producer and the Creator of "Star Trek"

"We have to continually be jumping off cliffs and developing our wings on the way down."

—Kurt Vonnegut

"Creativity takes courage."

—Henri Matisse

IF SUMMER LEARNING LOSS IS THE PROBLEM, SUMMER LEARNING ACTIVITIES ARE THE SOLUTION!

Away from the tests and the pressures of the regular school year, the summer months can be a special time for parents and educators to try something new and special:

❑ For parents and children, summer is a great time to be creative. Read new books, play new games, visit libraries and museums and parks that you've never been to.

❑ For teachers and principals, summer is the time to innovate. Create new summer programs and new ways to reach students.

❑ For school administrators and school reformers, summer is the time to introduce new programs. Free of the constraints that dictate so many practices and policies during the school year, summer is a great time to create programs that allow teachers to teach in new and different ways. You can train new teachers who need classroom experience, experiment with classroom technology, or create programs around subjects like music, art, science and social studies, which never seem to get enough time during the school year. Think of the summer months as a "laboratory for school reform and improvement."

By fostering innovation, summer programs have the potential to lead to breakthrough approaches that can eventually be implemented during the academic year. Here are some great examples of major innovations that started as tiny programs during the summer months:

NYC's "School of One"

New York City's School of One, a middle-school mathematics program lauded as "the future of education" by the former president of Teacher's College at Columbia University, grew out of a $1 million summer pilot program launched in 2009. Now operating in six schools across three New York City boroughs, School of One has become a model for using technology to develop personalized instructional experiences that are adjusted daily based on the individual student's learning style.

Harlem RBI

Harlem RBI's DREAM Charter School was born out of an innovative summer program providing inner-city youth with opportunities to play, learn, and grow through the power of team sports. It is hailed today as a model of the potential for summer learning innovations to reinvent school-year education.

Since its founding in 1991 as a summer program, Harlem RBI has grown to serve more than 1,700 boys and girls ages 5–22 annually in both East Harlem and the South Bronx, providing them with year-round sports, educational and enrichment activities. More than a school or a set of educational services, Harlem RBI also provides affordable housing units and a year-round community center. Rich Berlin, Founder and CEO, says,

> *"It all started as a small summer program, because summer is the time of year when we had the freedom to innovate."*

Dartmouth University

At Dartmouth, one of the world's most elite universities, all sophomores are required to take courses on campus during the summer. For the Ivy League institution, summer learning isn't just about safeguarding the intellectual investment it makes from September to June; it's also about the efficient use of space. Dartmouth instituted the unusual plan after going coed in 1972. With the influx of female students, it was no longer economically feasible to leave school buildings vacant for three months every year. While Dartmouth has figured it out, tens of thousands of public K-12 schools lay dormant over the summer in an era of scarce resources.

FUND INNOVATION!

For 22 years Margaret McKenna served as president of Lesley University in Cambridge, Massachusetts, which runs one of the nation's largest and best recognized graduate programs for teachers, principals and superintendents. She also served as undersecretary of the U.S. Department of Education. After retiring from her position at Lesley, McKenna moved into one of the most visible positions in U.S. philanthropy–running the charitable efforts of retail behemoth Wal-Mart Stores as head of the Walmart Foundation.

Charged with directing close to $1 billion in cash and in-kind contributions for the world's largest private employer, McKenna looked closely at how the foundation could steer its considerable financial heft to maximize impact. "We wanted to do something about the achievement gap," she says, "and as I learned more, I came to the conclusion that the opportunity with the most leverage, and where we should put most of our money in K-12, was summer learning. It's inexpensive, and the payback is so high."

While a small number of other national foundations have prioritized investments in summer learning (Wallace, David and Lucile Packard, New York Life and JP Morgan Chase, for example), most have largely ignored the issue. Consider that:

❑ Summer rarely features in the workshops and sessions of major education conferences;

❏ Less than half largest education foundations in the US have an explicit summer portfolio;

❏ In one recent year, less than 2% of the 51,000 philanthropic grants made in education included any support for summer learning.

PROGRAMS WORK!

Now more than ever, a sizeable and growing number of educators, policy-makers and, importantly, parents, are familiar with the problem of summer learning loss and engaged in the search for effective interventions. Indeed, there is a significant body of evidence showing that high quality summer programs promote learning, curb summer learning loss and are cost-effective.

Big Data, Brain Research and the Future of Summer Learning

"I [am] struck by how important measurement is to improving the human condition. You can achieve incredible progress if you set a clear goal and find a measure that will drive progress toward that goal."

—Bill Gates

"Measurement is the first step that leads to control and eventually to improvement. If you can't measure something, you can't understand it. If you can't understand it, you can't control it. If you can't control it, you can't improve it."

**—H. James Harrington,
author and management consultant**

By now, hopefully, you're on board with the fact that summer learning loss is serious business and that summer learning can make a difference in a big way. But there is much work to be done. Let's pause to consider some of the fascinating research that's happening, what's still left to be done, and what you can do as you become more empowered with good information.

WE KNOW A LOT, BUT WE DON'T KNOW ENOUGH...

First, knowledge is power, as they say, so here's my argument for the areas in which we need to learn much more. As I discussed in Chapters One and Two, we know a great deal about summer learning loss. We know, for instance, that during the summer months, children in the early elementary grades can lose as much as 25 percent of what they've learned during the school year. We also know that summer learning loss can occur summer after summer after summer, and the cumulative effect of these annual losses constitute a major drag on achievement and a significant cause of the achievement gap between middle-class and lower income students. Finally, we know that the extent of summer learning loss varies by child, by family circumstances, by grade level and by subject area.

Despite all that we know, many important questions still have yet to be asked, let alone answered. One big challenge we face right now is that we don't understand the variety of situations experienced by students, and the way that these situations impact summer learning loss. The more we can understand about students' unique experiences, the better we can support all youth.

Students in Special Education
To begin, we need to better understand and measure the extent of summer learning loss experienced by students in special education. Roughly 10

percent of American students receive special education services and many of them are our most vulnerable students. The term "special education" covers a range of learning related issues—for example, I received special education services because of a speech defect in first and second grades.

In general, we know that children in special education tend to learn at a different pace and, sometimes, in a different style than students in "regular education." These students might be particularly susceptible to extreme summer learning loss, yet researchers and educators have almost no data on this.

High School Students

Secondly, researchers rarely measure summer learning loss among high school students. While we can assume that summer learning loss is different for older students than it is for elementary school students, we need to understand which students are at risk and in what subjects. If we don't understand the problem, then we can't craft programs and policies to support our high school students.

English Language Learners

We know almost nothing about the degree of summer learning loss experienced by our large and growing population of English Language Learners. When I taught elementary school in New York City, almost all of my students were either immigrants or the children of immigrants. They spoke Spanish in their homes and neighborhoods. Many of these students were exposed to very little English during the summer months when schools were closed, and it's likely that their verbal and written English language skills declined. Unfortunately, there are no studies that measure summer learning loss amongst English language learners. This fact is particularly surprising given their increase as a percentage of the population, as well as the underachievement and high dropout rates of Latino students in general.

Children Living in Rural Areas

Finally, researchers and the foundations that support them have largely ignored the summer experiences of children living in rural areas, many of whom are growing up in poverty. This is beginning to change, as a small number of researchers are now turning their attention to rural areas, but it is essential that we increase our understanding of these students and the programs that serve them, all of which must grapple with the difficult and expensive problem of long distance transportation.

While there is still a lot that we don't know yet, there are some promising new possibilities for understanding the unique challenges that each child faces during the summer months; as I discuss below, I'm hopeful that big data and brain research will soon yield important breakthroughs.

THE PROMISE OF BIG DATA

"In big data lies the potential for revolutionizing, well, everything."
—Elaine Grant, Harvard School of Public Health

The emergence of "big data" provides a unique opportunity for parents, educators and policymakers. "Big data" is a term used to describe massive sets of data that are generated by millions of rs. Consider the information captured by online math programs such as BedtimeMath.org or FirstinMath.com, as well as online reading programs such as PBSKids.org and StoryJumper.com.

These programs, and many others like them, are used year-round by millions of students across all fifty states. Every time a student logs-on and completes a problem, a usage record is generated that includes whether the student solved the problem correctly, as well as the level at which the student is performing. By analyzing this data, educators can begin to pinpoint with great accuracy which skills are most susceptible to summer learning loss, and what types of practice are most effective at keeping skills up.

BRAIN RESEARCH

"There's never been a more exciting moment in neuroscience than now."
**—Gary Marcus,
Co-Editor of The Future of the Brain:
Essays by the World's Leading Neuroscientists**

Have you seen images of MRI scans in which parts of the brain "light up" in brightly colored reds and yellows as patients perform tasks that activate specific areas of their brains? Neuroscientists are using these "brain mapping" techniques to identify the structures in the brain that are associated with particular functions. For instance, researchers at the University of Washington are mapping infants' brains as they develop new skills, while researchers at the National Institutes of Health are studying the brains of Alzheimer's patients as they lose or "forget" knowledge they acquired decades earlier.

Neuroscientists may soon be able to use these brain mapping techniques to help parents and educators better understand and prevent summer learning loss. The technology exists, for example, to study the types of knowledge that are most susceptible to summer learning loss. Researchers could also investigate whether the teaching method by which children learn a particular set of skills during the school year affects their ability to retain information through the summer.

Our challenge now is to build support for these types of research programs so that we can learn as quickly as possible about what happens to children's brains during the months when they are away from schooling.

USING RESEARCH EVIDENCE TO
IMPROVE LEARNING

Why is all this information so important? Because educators and policy-makers need evidence-based guidance in order to craft effective policy and programs. Just as we invest in medical research to find treatment and cures for disease, we need to invest in educational research to find a "cure" for summer learning loss. In this case, the "cure" will not be a single, one-size-fits-all program, but rather a set of programs and policies that are supported by the general public and customized for the unique needs of specific children and their families and communities.

As a starting point, it is critically important that data on summer learning loss become more widely available. Parents, teachers, principals and superintendents need to know exactly how much loss is experienced by children in their own homes, classrooms, and schools. Some students will experience extreme summer loss in one subject area but not in others; some students will experience loss in one grade but not in subsequent grades. Ultimately, we want educators to offer customized learning opportunities that are crafted for the specific needs of each student. To provide this, teachers and principals need to measure and understand summer learning loss among their own students.

How do we get schools, districts, and states across the country to take action? It's one thing for teachers, principals and superintendents to read about summer learning loss in a book or journal article that cites research conducted in another city or state, but it's quite another thing for educators to see firsthand the toll that summer learning loss takes on <u>their own students</u>. When this happens, parents, educators and policymakers will begin to make big changes in their own communities.

THE FUTURE OF SUMMER LEARNING LOSS: AN EPIDEMIC OR THE MISSING LINK?

A friend of mine once described summer learning loss as an "epidemic." "Think about it," he argued:

> "Millions of American children experience it on an annual basis. It damages their academic performance by dragging down their skills and test scores. Moreover, it hits poor kids the hardest, and it costs taxpayers tens of millions of dollars a year in lost learning."

It's a persuasive argument and, in fact, he may be right. Indeed, I suspect that if we used the word epidemic, summer learning loss might finally get the attention it needs.

But let's stop for a moment. Let's pause to consider how we might turn this negative trend into a powerful tool for positive change. Rather than describing summer learning loss as an epidemic, let's think of summer learning (without the loss) as "the missing link." Chronologically speaking, summer is the time period that links one school year to the next. Metaphorically, and perhaps more importantly, it is the link between learning and forgetting, between achievement and underachievement. Our challenge is to transform "the missing link" into a period of fun learning and engagement. This transformation can only happen once we begin to change the way that we think about summertime.

IT'S LIKE WEARING A BIKE HELMET
OR STRAPPING ON YOUR SEATBELT

How can you help make the change in your community? Transforming something that we've always done the same way may seem like a monumental task. But it doesn't have to be. In fact, we've done it many times before. For instance, when I was a kid in the 1970's nobody wore bike helmets. Today, every kid wears a bike helmet and countless millions of serious injuries have been prevented.

Dr. David Kessler, the renowned former head of the Food and Drug Administration, led the nation's fight against smoking. He describes public health victories like the ones to curb smoking, stop drunk driving, and require the use of seatbelts as massive "cultural shifts." Currently engaged in the battle to curb obesity, particularly childhood obesity, Dr. Kessler makes this argument:

"If you look at the great public health successes, if you look at tobacco, if you look at seatbelts – how did we win those battles? Sure there's a role for government, I mean, in part. But in the end what did we do? We changed the way we look at tobacco. We changed the way [we look at seatbelts] – I get in the car and I don't feel normal unless I put on that seatbelt. So yes, government has a role, the industry has a role, we as consumers have a role. But the first thing is we have to change how we look at [it]."

—**David Kessler**

In other words, it is up to us as parents and teachers to think about our summers in a dramatically new and different way – and then to push our leaders and elected officials to change their thinking.

(10)

Conclusion:

It's America vs. The World

With an average of 180 days in the school year, the U.S. has one of the shortest school years—and longest summer breaks—in the developed world. By way of comparison, the South Korean school year is 220 days long; the Japanese school year is 242 days long.

"OUR NATION IS AT RISK." So warned a blue-ribbon presidential panel in a landmark report on the state of education in the United States. Members of the National Commission on Excellence in Education rendered their verdict at the outset of the 36-page report, and its conclusion about American education wasn't pretty:

> *Our once unchallenged preeminence in commerce, industry, science, and technological innovation is being overtaken by competitors throughout the world ... The educational foundations of our society are presently being eroded by a rising tide of mediocrity that threatens our very future as a Nation and a people ... If an unfriendly foreign power had attempted to impose on America the mediocre educational performance that exists today, we might well have viewed it as an act of war. As it stands, we have allowed this to happen to ourselves ... We have, in effect, been committing an act of unthinking, unilateral educational disarmament.*

Those words likely resonate with anyone familiar with today's schools. But guess what-that report was issued in 1983!

THE PROMISE OF AMERICAN EDUCATION

For all of its flaws, the public education system in the United States has been essential to the vision of America as the land of opportunity. Our system of free, compulsory public education was the world's first. Beginning in the middle of the 19th century, when reformers successfully pushed for free elementary education for everyone, the notion that the child of a migrant farmworker is entitled to the same schooling as the child of a wealthy business executive has been embedded in our national identity.

So why can't we fix the problem of underachievement in America? To be sure, we've tried many things. Seemingly every political candidate, Democrat or Republican, has argued that we must assign the highest priority to improving our schools. Over the years we watched as one President Bush announced his intention to be the Education President and then saw his son introduce major education-reform legislation, The No Child Left Behind Act, as the first significant act of his presidency. Under President Obama, we have witnessed efforts at bold new initiatives in Race to the Top and Common Core State Standards.

Along the way reform advocates have promoted a laundry list of solutions: improving teacher quality, reducing class size, putting computers in every classroom, increasing parental involvement, ending social promotion, pushing character education, and redoubling our focus on STEM (Science, Technology, Education and Math). Many of these are smart and important ideas. Some have been implemented. But our schools still fail to meet our expectations.

Meanwhile, we've paid little attention to the problem of summer learning loss. By focusing only on the fall, winter and spring while ignoring the loss that millions of children experience every June, July, and August, we have undercut our own efforts are reform and improvement.

The problem of summer learning loss is the most neglected cause of underachievement in America.

POLICYMAKERS, SCHOOL DISTRICTS, AND SCHOOLS OF EDUCATION NEED TO "OWN" THE PROBLEM OF SUMMER LEARNING LOSS

"Summertime needs to be prioritized as a key context in which declines in academics and health can and must be addressed."

—Researchers Amy Bohnert, Nicole Zarrett, and Amy Heard

Parents and teachers can turn summer learning loss into summer learning gains if they have the necessary awareness, tools, and support. Policymakers and institutions of education also need to step up and do a much better job "owning" the problem of summer learning loss. Consider, for example, that the colleges and universities that train our teachers have largely ignored the problem of summer learning loss—in most programs, there is not a single course offered on the subject, and most education textbooks ignore it as well. In addition, there is virtually no federal funding dedicated to summer learning and almost no federal funding for research on summer learning loss.

While some states and districts are working hard to find solutions to summer learning loss, most have yet to tackle this in any serious way. We see evidence of this all the time. While millions of dollars are spent every year on issues like teacher quality and curriculum, only a tiny percentage of education dollars are spent on summer learning – even though surveys and other studies show increasing parental demand for high quality and affordable summer programs. As an example, I recently read about a large urban district with an annual school budget of $1 billion. The school board was debating whether to spend $4 million or $6 million on a summer program; in other words, district leaders were reluctant to spend even 1/5 of 1 percent of their budget on a problem that impacted nearly all their students. Unfortunately, this kind of response (or non-response) is all too typical.

THE GOOD NEWS...

The good news is that in small towns and big cities across the country, the momentum is building to increase summer learning opportunities for all students. In 2015, an analysis by the National Summer Learning Association found that more than 100 bills to support summer programming had been introduced in state legislatures. At least 15 of these bills specifically included appropriations totaling more than $130 million. More than 160 state and community coalitions have prioritized summer learning as a key strategy for improving third-grade reading proficiency as part of the Campaign for Grade-Level Reading.

CELEBRATE SUMMER LEARNING DAY!

On June 19, 2015, nonprofit organizations, school districts, mayors, and libraries hosted more than 700 community events as part of Summer Learning Day, an annual advocacy day led by the National Summer Learning Association to raise awareness of summer slide and the importance of summer programs that are enjoyable, educational, and accessible to all families. For the second consecutive year, First Lady Michelle Obama delivered a video message of support for the effort. We also know that more parents are interested in having opportunities available for their children.

In 2016, Summer Learning Day will be celebrated on July 14–and promises to be the biggest one ever. For more information, or to highlight your favorite program, visit www.SummerLearning.org.

STILL THE LAND OF OPPORTUNITY

Today, public schools in the United States educate 50 million children. The promise is clear: Through hard work and good grades, anyone from any social or economic standing can parlay education into a prosperous and fulfilling life. Despite its struggles, public schooling is still widely held to be the best way for our capitalist, meritocratic society to level the playing field by providing everyone with a fair chance to succeed.

Our commitment to public education is one of which we should be proud. But we also need to make sure that the best efforts of students, parents, and educators during the school year are not lost each and every summer. The consequences of summer learning loss impact not only individuals, but families, communities, and the country as a whole. In order for our public education system to deliver on the promise of success for all students, regardless of their background, we need to commit ourselves to the notion that "summers matter."

IN CONCLUSION, WE AMERICANS LOVE OUR SUMMERS—AND WE SHOULD!

Can we continue to love and enjoy our summers while keeping our kids learning during the summer?

The short answer is ... YES!

And the longer answer is ... Yes, we can AND we must. America has a long history of finding solutions and fixing wrongs. Educational leadership and innovation are part of our social fabric – and it's that energy and determination that will allow us to embrace summer learning. We owe it to our children—all of our children.

POP-QUIZ

Directions: Circle the correct answer.

My goals for the summer are:

A. To keep reading
B. To practice math
C. To eat healthy, sleep well, and exercise
D. To have fun
E. All of the Above!

Your FREE Guide to Summer Learning

(TIP: Print the checklist at the end of this chapter and tape it someplace visible – like your fridge. You can use it all summer long.)

STEP ONE: BEGIN BEFORE THE BEGINNING

In other words, plan ahead. That way, you and your family are ready for summer learning before school lets out. The 20–2-1 Summer Challenge is a simple and fun tool – and here are ten more suggestions to help you get started:

Talk to your child's teacher about summer learning:

❑ 1. Ask for a summer homework packet.
❑ 2. Ask for a summer reading list.
❑ 3. Ask for recommendations for high-quality online programs. If your teacher used an online reading or math program during the school year, ask if it will be available throughout the summer.

Talk to your child's principal, assistant principal, or guidance counselor about summer learning:

❏ 4. Ask if the school library will be open during the summer.

❏ 5. Ask if the school or school district offers any summer programs.

❏ 6. If your child receives special education services during the school year, ask what services will be available during the summer.

❏ 7. If your child is eligible for the free or reduced-price lunch program, ask if meals will be served during the summer and when and where.

Research what's available (and affordable) in your community:

❏ 8. Most libraries have a free summer reading program with prizes and rewards for children who read throughout the summer. They often have free organized activities as well. If your child doesn't already have a library card, sign him or her up for one. They're free!

❏ 9. Check with local non-profit organizations like the Boys and Girls Club, park districts, and the YMCA – most run camps throughout the summer. Some programs may be low-cost or free.

Consider what's already in your home and neighborhood:

❏ 10. Look for toys, books, puzzles and board games that you already own – children often enjoy playing with "old favorites" that they haven't seen in a while; and explore the playgrounds, parks, walking trails, and libraries in your community.

STEP TWO: SCHOOL'S OUT-NOW WHAT?

Let the fun begin. And, yes, learning can be fun. Summer is the perfect time for children to learn and explore in new and exciting ways – and ALL of these activities can be included in the 20–2-1 Summer Challenge.

Read. Read. Read.

❑ 1. Summer reading should be FUN reading! Help your child read ANYTHING AND EVERYTHING that interests him or her. A great way to get started is by celebrating the end of the school year with a special trip to the library or a bookstore. Help your child set-up a comfortable and quiet space with good lighting for summer reading. Encourage your child to create a schedule for daily reading and set an example by letting your child see you read every day.

Practice Math.

❑ 2. Find creative ways to practice math: ask your child to help you tally the bill at the grocery store, calculate time, or follow a recipe. Some children enjoy math workbooks or online worksheets – there are lots of free ones.

Turn off the TV! Turn off the screens!

❑ 3. A little bit of screen time is ok – but too much screen time is not healthy. Monitor (and limit) screen time in the summertime as well as during the school year.

Make Art!

❏ 4. Kids love art projects of every kind – but they rarely have enough time during the school year to draw and paint and construct as much as they'd like. Picasso said, "Every child is an artist. The problem is how to remain one once we grow up." Let the summer months be the time when your child discovers that he or she has the amazing ability to create through art.

Experiment! Do Science!

❏ 5. Watch an ice cube melt. Grow grass. Play with magnets. Collect rocks. Collect leaves. Summer is a great time to experiment with science.

Eat smart. Eat healthy.

❏ 6. It's ok to eat ice cream on a hot summer day – but don't eat only ice cream. Kids need help eating healthy. Without the structure of the school day, some kids tend to eat tons of junk food during the summer. Keep plenty of fresh fruits and veggies at the ready, like carrot and celery sticks with hummus, ranch dressing or peanut butter for "skinny dipping". Process watermelon in your blender and freeze it in popsicle forms for an icy, refreshing treat.

Get outside. Take a hike. Play in the sun. Go for a bike ride or a run. Visit a park.

❏ 7. Some children experience unhealthy levels of weight gain during the summer months because they get less exercise when schools are closed. It's important to help your child stay physically active all summer long.

Go to a museum – again and again.

❏ 8. For every child with an interest, there is a museum with a special collection. Insects? Space travel? The ocean? Art? History? Find a museum and visit it – whether in person or online.

Read a poem.

❏ 9. Here's the start of a silly, ridiculous, funny, poem by Shel Silverstein:
    Millie McDeevit screamed a scream
    So loud it make her eyebrows steam.
    She screamed so loud her jawbone broke,
    Her tongue caught fire, her nostrils smoked…

This is just one of a thousand wonderful poems for children. Google "funny poems for children" and see which ones your child enjoys. Read them aloud. Memorize a line or two. Substitute words to make your own rhymes. Ask your child to describe the poem in their own words means and what it means.

Finally … go to sleep!

❏ 10. Keep a bedtime routine. It's ok for your child to stay up a bit later in the summer but it's still very important to maintain a regular bedtime and routine. For example, if you read a bedtime story to your child during the school year, then read a bedtime story during the summer.

STEP THREE: BACK TO SCHOOL

It's not enough to prevent learning loss for just one summer. Next summer also matters. So does the summer after that, and the summer after that, and on and on.

Start planning for next summer.

❏ 1. September is a great time to reflect on what worked and what didn't work over the summer. Write down your thoughts, and use this checklist to think about what you want to do next summer.

Be an activist.

❏ 2. Talk to other parents in your child's school and to leaders in your community about summer learning loss. Work to keep your school library open during the summer and work to build support for low-cost summer enrichment programs for the children in your neighborhood, city or town.

My Summer Matters!

The 20-2-1 Summer Challenge

OVERVIEW

The "20-2-1" Summer Challenge is a simple tool for you to support your child's learning during the summer months.

The Challenge consists of three elements:

- **20** minutes of reading every day;
- **2** "choice" activities each day; and
- **1** math game (or activity) each day.

A couple of key points:

- When it comes to reading, it's OK to read with your child or to read aloud to your child; if your child is older, he or she can read anything they find interesting.

– The "choice" activities should be fun ones that your child selects for himself or herself (see next page for details).

– When it comes to math, remember that your job is NOT to teach your child algebra or trigonometry over the summer. Rather, you simply need to help your child practice his or her math skills.

– Give yourself some flexibility. Do the Challenge five days a week, not seven-and it's fine if you miss a day or two occasionally.

– Be creative. It's fine to adapt the Challenge to your family's unique circumstances and interests.

The next few pages will help you get started:

<u>Step 1</u>: Set your goals for the summer.

<u>Step 2</u>: Identify helpful resources in your home and community.

<u>Step 3</u>: Take the "20–2-1 Summer Challenge" and track your progress all summer long.

STEP 1: SET YOUR GOALS
FOR THE SUMMER

Read for at least 20 Minutes Every Day.

It's OK to read with your child or to read aloud to your child if they're not yet reading on their own. Let your child read anything that interests him or her. For example:

A comic book. A cookbook. A newspaper article. Something online. Something on paper. A novel. A graphic novel. A sports magazine. A nature magazine. A silly poem. A serious poem. A book about art. A book about history. A book about the history of art.

Each Day, Pick 2 "Choice" Activities.

- ○ The "choice" activities should be fun ones that your child selects for himself or herself
- ○ Make ART: Color. Draw. Paint. Shape clay. Construct.
- ○ Experiment! Do Science!
- ○ Exercise: swim, take a hike, play in the sun, go for a bike ride, go for a walk, visit a park.
- ○ Go to a museum.
- ○ Write in a journal.
- ○ Use a computer to write in Word, do math in Excel, or create a slideshow in PowerPoint.

❍ Attend a camp.
❍ Take a trip.
❍ Turn off the TV! (FOR THE WHOLE DAY!)
❍ Other suggestions:_____

Do 1 Math Game (or Activity) Every Day.
Your job is NOT to teach your child algebra or trigonometry over the summer. Simply help your child practice his or her math skills. Each math game or activity should last about 10 minutes. Here are some examples:

❍ Calculate the cost of two or more items in the supermarket.
❍ Play a game like Math 24.
❍ Learn to code for free at KhanAcademy.org.
❍ Follow a recipe.
❍ Count money.
❍ Practice multiplication facts. Count backwards.
❍ My Summer Matters!
❍ The 20–2-1 Summer Challenge

STEP 2: IDENTIFY HELPFUL RESOURCES IN YOUR HOME AND COMMUNITY

What resources in your home and community can help your child meet the 20–2-1 Summer Challenge? Circle all that are available.

In your home:

Children's books.

Newspapers, magazines or cookbooks.

A computer with PowerPoint, Excel, or Word.

An internet connection.

A book of poems.

A calculator.

What else:_____

In your community:

Your school's library (is it open?)

Your school's playground.

A public library.

A public park.

A nearby swimming pool.

A museum.

What else: _____

STEP 3: TAKE THE 20-2-1 SUMMER CHALLENGE AND TRACK YOUR PROGRESS ALL SUMMER LONG!

Wednesday, June 15th, 2016

The 1st Day of My Summer

20 Today I read for _____ minutes.

2 Today I completed these "choice" activities:

    1. _____

    2. _____

1 Today I played this math game: _____

Thursday, June 16th, 2016

The 2nd Day of My Summer

20 Today I read for _____ minutes.

2 Today I completed these "choice" activities:

    1. _____

    2. _____

1 Today I played this math game: _____

Friday, June 17th, 2016

The 3rd Day of My Summer

20 Today I read for _____ minutes.

2 Today I completed these "choice" activities:

    1. _____

    2. _____

1 Today I played this math game: _____

WEEKLY PLANNER

Circle the days that you completed the 20–2-1 Challenge

June 13, the 1st week of summer:
M T W Th F Sa Su

June 20, the 2nd week of summer:
M T W Th F Sa Su

June 27, the 3rd week of summer:
M T W Th F Sa Su

July 4, the 4th week of summer:
M T W Th F Sa Su

July 11, the 5th week of summer:
M T W Th F Sa Su

July 18, the 6th week of summer:
M T W Th F Sa Su

July 25, the 7th week of summer:
M T W Th F Sa Su

August 1, the 8th week of summer:
M T W Th F Sa Su

August 8, the 9th week of summer:
M   T   W   Th   F   Sa   Su

August 15, the 10th week of summer:
M   T   W   Th   F   Sa   Su

August 22, the 11th week of summer:
M   T   W   Th   F   Sa   Su

August 29, the 12th week of summer:
M   T   W   Th   F   Sa   Su

September 5, the 13th week of summer:
M   T   W   Th   F   Sa   Su

NOW COUNT ALL THE CIRCLED DAYS.

HOW MANY DAYS DID YOU PRACTICE LEARNING THIS SUMMER?

The End

(almost)

Here's the last thing I want to say:

By encouraging your kids to be learners in every season, you're teaching them to be learners for life – and that's a very special lesson.

Finally, being a parent isn't always easy (even during summer vacation), but your love, support, and encouragement are the most important and wonderful gifts you can give your child–and that's true whether it's winter, spring, summer or fall!

The End

(for real this time)

FOR FURTHER READING

Since the late 1960s', an interdisciplinary group of sociologists, psychologists, statisticians, program evaluators, and policy analysts have employed qualitative and quantitative methods to investigate summer learning from a variety of perspectives. My goal in writing this book has been to "translate" the most important research findings into everyday language that offers practical information for parents and teachers.

For readers who seek additional information, the following websites can be helpful:

The National Summer Learning Association
www.summerlearning.org

The RAND Corporation's Report, "Making Summer Count"
http://www.rand.org/pubs/monographs/MG1120.html

The U.S. Department of Agriculture's Summer Food Service Program
http://www.fns.usda.gov/sfsp/summer-food-service-program-sfsp